# about this

bonnie tobias

Photos and text Copyright © 2025 by bonnie tobias

All rights reserved. This book may not be reproduced or stored in
whole or in part by any means without the written permission
of the author except for brief quotations for the purpose of review.

ISBN: 978-1-963569-85-8 (Hard Cover)
       978-1-963569-86-5 (Soft Cover)

tobias. bonnie
about this

Edited by: Amy Ashby and Hanah Cohen



Published by Warren Publishing
Charlotte, NC
www.warrenpublishing.net
Printed in the United States

for the ancients
always close
always within

# about this
## the poetry

this collection gives voice to the things that often go unsaid; the shared realities of pain and suffering that accompany a life. it explores the effects of childhood exposure to parental depression; the complexities of relationships; the pull of things, place, and memory; and the inner workings of anxiety, silencing, and aging. here is poetry that treats suffering not as something to be ignored, but as something to share, thereby bringing about connection and solace. i hope each reader can find a thread to help pull them along, a few words of communion that will comfort and lift.

# about this
## the invitation

these poems now ask
what will you find in us?
where will you take us?

finding the worth of a poem is easy; its meaning exists solely between the reader and the words. think of the last time you shared a video of your cat or a new song, face-to-face, with a good friend. at times there can be a bit of a hiccup, a moment when your initial energy gets lost in transmission. your friend doesn't "get it" quite the way you did. this doesn't indicate that the song or the cat or your friend or you are wrong. it simply demonstrates that everyone gets something different out of everything, and that, dear reader, is the ease of poetry! a poem simply looks for the answer that is written in your heart.

here's how to find your poetic treasure: read slow or fast. read the first line only, the entire poem, or skip to the end. read and re-read. take a breath. listen to the way your body reacts (stomach, heartbeat, feet). is there a word or two, or a line, that tickles the back of your neck or begs you to stop and swallow? if so, this is the gift!

as you collect a phrase or a few words, hold on to them. feel free to memorize them, jot them down, underline, or tear them from the pages of this book (don't do this if the book belongs to your friend!). you have now met the poetry. you've unlocked the special meaning that was waiting among the words. gracefully place your gift in your pocket. take it with you.

life is a blast, and life holds suffering. i hope you find your unique present within the poetry. may it ride along with your happiness and sit close to you when it's dark. may it be with you forever.

# about this
## the process

i was placed in this world along the margin of here and gone. living as an in-between has given me a heart-and-soul space for the deposit of pain and suffering. like a net cast into the sea, part of me drifts freely until some reality of a person, place, encounter, or memory becomes a truth i must carry and write about.

i don't know what the world will need to drop into this space. i don't ask or intuit the unfolding. when the net is tugged, i get a bit heavier. i sink and spin with the hurt and trials that always accompany a life. many of my poems come from the snagged realities of family, love, strangers, and aging. along the way, i also try to sort out my floaty, tangled inner self. my poetry is often born of remembrance and the present state of mind and body.

the loads of life are to be carried. this is our common reality. i put pen to paper to give voice and acknowledgment to this struggle.

# about this
# the poems

poems for you ............................................... 6
atlanto-occipital joint................................... 7
yours to bear .................................................. 8
after mid-day ................................................. 9
quiet, quiet cataract ..................................... 10
a-frame ........................................................... 11
dust .................................................................. 12
further along ................................................. 13
those tears ...................................................... 14
forsaken .......................................................... 17
gold star days ................................................ 18
about you ....................................................... 20
a trip home..................................................... 21
wrong turn ..................................................... 22
take it back .................................................... 23
silent '67.......................................................... 25
alone in the dark .......................................... 27
and again ....................................................... 28
sturdy .............................................................. 29
delightful ....................................................... 30
hammering down the clouds ..................... 32
not here ........................................................... 33
lady captain ................................................... 34
moon tan ........................................................ 35
too old for tea parties................................... 36
swollen ............................................................ 37
before natalie goldberg ............................... 39
withered. gone. ............................................. 41
claire's flash fiction ...................................... 42
friday ............................................................... 43
my idol ............................................................ 44

## poems for you

i keep writing
poems for you

an attempt to resurrect

the dead creases
of your mind

where thought
and memory
no longer reside

an ischemia

has crept
into the valley
of remembrance

severing the tendrils
of our relationship

now disjointed

you practice
alone

your feet
unbalanced

your speech
unuttered

your self
a lost recollection

at this point
the written word

only soothes
the writer

# atlanto-occipital joint: variation on a definition

at the base of the skull
a sharp, metal rim
sits on a rod
of once thick rebar
now twisted
stiff with age

surrounding this union
of pivot
and edge

deranged
connective tissue
reshaped
into rusted shrapnel

the nuts and bolts
of life—
a pinched mess

throughout the night
house
and human form

creak
in dreams
and labor

## yours to bear

it was the look
in the stranger's eye

the original assignment
of suffering

the authentic knowledge
*this is never going away*

it's mine
it's yours
ours to manage

never eradicate

ours to return
to the rivers
and soil

## after mid-day

i am fashioned
from earth and light

an eternal union
a brilliant divide

infinite and definitive
bracketed by breath

and what of this hushed
mostly silent soul

she
lives within the shoreline
of sleep's saturation

the slow
gentle
roll

she has the freedom
to wander
circle and sing
laugh and dance

i've been napping
while the

tomatoes
slowly ripen

## quiet, quiet cataract

you blink
enough times
and a thick shell forms

an eye-pearl
floating
in the fovea

proof
of our pure
origin

the sea

marine blue-green
kelpish brown
misty
mysterious gray

each
mixed with a glint
of golden sand

as life pulls you closer
to the ancient veil

my own layering
begins—

in a sacred
perfect
pool of shaping

we fuse

you become
the rarest of gems

sea-worthy

once again

## a-frame

we tried the loop
tied love's loop
pressed back into time
a single unit

i have circled your breath
felt my heart
beat
dull
and
full
upon its lull and lift

you set an orbit
around and
through

my thoughts, my hands
slightly
almost
always
open

we've become home
even as
the journey
toward it
accelerates

we are beings
who carry the load

one light touch
our steady framework

we tied the loop
pressed back-to-back
and still remain
supported

### dust

i glance
at the idea
of swiping
layers
away

quickly
change course

laundry room
hangers
now
sorted
by
style
color
size

## further along

each night
from now until

forever

since yesterday
and before

weary heads
find
a pillow
a spot
or simply
nod off

eyes closed in discontent
shuttered
from the discontent

may the night
take you
a bit further along

bring you into the arms
of
acceptance
release
understanding

## those tears

they
were one more thing
never talked about

in the september rush
of books and sweaters
there was no place
for a crying
second grader

each morning
i became
an annoying complication

a crack
in the smooth veneer
of our family's
façade

my sisters were confused
they knew the drill

i was
uncool and red-eyed
cumbersome
as homework

mom was all business

here was
an additional task

something else
to be completed
efficiently

she just needed me
to stop

dad wasn't home
he left for the factory
early

one day—
a plastic bank appeared
shaped like a trashcan
bearing a restaurant logo

it must have been
pulled out
of a magic hat

fast food
was as frivolous
as name-brand clothes

we never ate there
never wore those

perhaps my mom
mentioned it
to a co-worker

they hatched a plan

if i didn't
act up
made it to school
without public display

i was given
a quarter
a deposit
for saving the day

i don't know
if this charm worked

somehow
i outgrew it

but
it didn't outgrow me

i wore it hidden
like an unwanted tattoo
a stamp
announcing shame
and weirdness

an itch
at the back of my brain
always questioning
the why
of my behavior

27 years later
sitting
alone and quiet

a good girl
in my own home

Grandma Opoka
appeared
*oh how i loved her!*

i could see her
as she was

navy housedress
rayon with a belted waist
tiny flower print

her forgiving smile
safe, ready arms
her body
a pillow

she placed
her hand in mine
pieces of a puzzle
no longer lost

my small-child self
lovingly addressed
finally understood

April 27th
1967

her funeral
my first

## forsaken

for the sake of peace
joy is put away

in quiet hours
the turn of rot
provokes
an exhausted sigh

for the sake of it all
language is plain
diminished

as if spoken
from the bottom
of
a
tightly
packed
barrel

eventually

the spirit is
forsaken

there are limits
constraints
and costly
compromise
everywhere

time
cannot catch the rain
nor learn to say
stop

it is
an eternal bonfire
of once-gay souls

## gold star days

craft
a gold star
for those days—

those days
when the most banal tasks
are alive and hungry

a circle
of newborn grackles
screeching
with open mouths

their downy fleece
so fiercely dark

you will be
bruised
blue

on those days
even while being
pecked
and punished

hold this
as your mantra

*time moves*

*merciful twilight*
*eventually appears*

*birdcall will fade*
*into settling*
*silence*

when the gift
of muted landscape
presses

against outside walls
and windows

stop

and carefully note

you
provided
sustenance

gave every
minute
drip
full attention

hair washed
unstyled

quilt and pillow
smoothed
upon tired linens

overly processed diet
rinsed down
with pure water

anything
is enough

anything

## about you

because of you

words
are meaningless

what the eyes behold
evades imprint

no taste or smell
i go without

anything held
is
vacuous

because of you
i lose all

sense

grounded to earth
i ride the sky

## a trip home

i have nothing to leave behind
no trinket
no treat
just a memory
a touch

the small parts of me that long to
cling to your hands
smell your skin
look into your eyes

i want to be

wrapped and held
in one single thread of you
endless
timeless
always known

## wrong turn

i turned to the wall
tuned out need
dialed down voice

quite the receiver
receptor of signals

my reply—

a broadcast
of grand
silence

background music
in the house
where i

tiptoed
and sidestepped an
invisible
tripwire of

love
and depression
sudden rage
and
stumble

i was small
and fresh

quick to call
the corner
safe

i was good
efficient
to the point
of unplug

click off

## take it back

no genius am i
for in my youth
i could not find
a way to bring you in

time eventually found us
pushed
at our backs

we crossed the threshold together
forced to endure
the stoic face of dementia

why did it take so long
why did it take such hurt
for me to conjure the words

when you lost yours
i found
mine

a situation
never bartered for

in fantasy
in daydream
i read the poetry
and
you finally
sweetly
approve

but if you understand
if you can
grasp meaning

then there is no decline

the prose and i
rendered useless
slump back to

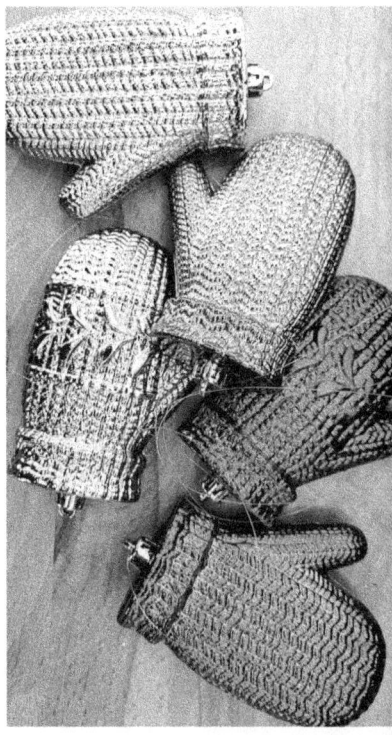

the beginning

the maddening cycle reminds us
the doorway
always
awaits

our fragile brilliance
forever eclipsed

by the time i was old enough
to reach you
you were too old to care

but i would surrender
the poem
abandon the praise
to keep the disease from you

# silent '67

april '67
gram's funeral
brisk scolding
*stop crying!*

emotions, needs, voice
all of me

shamed into
silence

july '67
riots
our house
artesian street
detroit

worried parents
upper peninsula
extended stay

chaos descended
radio, tv blared
city
burned in violence

will home still be there

adult voices
soundless
no explanation
no reassurance

frightened child remained
silent

a good girl

traumatic events
razed
reconstructed
my 7-year-old brain

september '67

monday
second grade
my heart stopped at
the door

for months i
shamefully cried before leaving

sisters embarrassed
parents frustrated
bribes to
stop—

discomfort
anguish
left unaddressed

the assumption
i'd outgrow
it

fifty years later

silence

deeply
attached
to
throat
and
bone

## alone in the dark

what is it
i ask

is there something i missed
something more

the clotted warm weight of night
is silent

an electric spiral of dis/ease

worms beneath my sternum
reaches
tingly
tarantula arms
around
ribs
and
wings

a door
believed open in
a dream

is not

this room
offers
no view
of the moon

## and again

again and again
i am the and
again

follower
feeler
compassion that pulls along

only fools believe
to channel
eases pain

involuntarily
this heart
carries
you

sinks
implores

how to breathe
again and again
through the slow bend of
existence

## sturdy

with one more condemnation
she goes silent

disinterested

exhausted

exhausted with running into the wall
she erects her own

this
is how empires
and strongholds
permanently
arise

how sweet division
saves

## delightful

afternoon nap

precipitated by
the magnetic sounds
of thunder

as i wake
i slowly

take in my world

a small house
by 2022 standards
but perfect for those
who were
almost

adults
in 1979

now
paper rustles in the kitchen
my ears dance

*Ron!*
*he's just down the hall—*

i shush and shoo
time away
break bread with the comfort
of a shared life

ignore the inevitable
expiration
of two beating hearts

ask whatever remains
to creep slowly
to the edge
of forecasted change

in a distant early evening
the coming storm
will have passed

one of us will wake—
ears stilled
perhaps even
momentarily confused

alone
in a new silence

fears no longer
settled in dreams
but rather
bursting
with reality

endlessly searching
for home

i roll over
loosen my thoughts
let my feet touch ground

*run toward Ron—*

## hammering down the clouds

truth is
when someone dies

we have no idea
how
or with whom

we'll ford
the path of pain

but trust this

it will feel
as if no other soul
has ever left the earth

for a while
this will be true

## not here

cursive or printed
no one would ever know

the letter was scribed
in dissolving ink

*i'm disappearing*
is what she'd written

could they see it now

long looks across the street
daydreams
apron strings
tied tight and high

while life's preciousness
lay bleating behind her

there would be
no backward glance
on this
or any other day

## lady captain

her vessel
rides filthy
and condemned

she straightens
two bath towels

sprays
the schmutz
off a pair of pants

perhaps tomorrow
the washwoman
will appear

## moon tan

on summer nights
under that luminous michigan sky

my sister and i
would moon tan

when our parents let us run the backyard
we'd twirl and dance within the showering beams

create towering shadows
watch them leap and fall upon the grass

the music was in our hearts
the bright rays
like water from a sprinkler

when we were stuck inside
upstairs and supposed to be asleep

we'd open the curtains
slowly raise the blinds
invite the planet in

we only had one window
my gosh
it was enough

we'd lie real still in our pjs
arms and legs out
like we'd seen
older girls and models do

in a strong square of light
we floated off the floor

we never questioned
the validity or wisdom
of getting a moon tan

we were so close
to knowing nothing

we knew
it all

## too old for tea parties

drained
like
a shot
of harsh
whiskey

the aftermath
of
friends

the incremental
exponential
tilt
and
tumble

the bright crescendo
the startling

souring

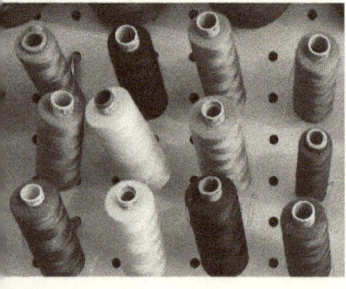

silencing of life—
shared

shared
slices
of pumpkin roll
milky, amber tea

passed
nibbled
complimented

gone

## swollen

human

filled with drops of bitter incantations
of a despised one

sung upon the crest
of each precious hour

hate habituated
spews behind
the sternal gladiolus

gums the articular surfaces of
spine and limb

wends down
into the pelvic girdle
(perhaps the privates itch)

too much
becomes
never enough

a dreadful condition

all that miserable
internal coupling
and
the next thing
one knows
(if one can know)

friends disengage
choose
not to reply

make no mention
of one's seemingly jaunty words

human

you've chosen to marry
to worship and hold
the source of your disdain

your beloved
has etched a new
profile
upon your once-smooth face

## before natalie goldberg

didn't realize

first
second
and third
thoughts

can appear
while writing

*for example*

i'm hungry
need breakfast
another cup of coffee

coffee (first thought)

¼ caff (second)

because
i don't want you
thinking
i'm hooked
on a stimulant

*ugh*
*okay*

first thought
coffee

second
¼ caff

3rd
stimulant *(to avoid repeat use of the word caffeine)*

or
is stimulant
the second thought of
¼ caff

*are you still with me*

*you can leave*
*if*

*you want*

*i'm going*
*to eat*

## withered. gone.

regret
reaches in

and pulls
the sternal post out
sideways

rib
broad muscle
pearly gray cartilage

yanked aside
like an invasive
garden pest

root and all

the heart chamber
is soundless
bloodless
vacant

claws
and long
yellowed teeth
savagely protect
her shame
and sadness

a life unsung

crouching
hiding

in the void

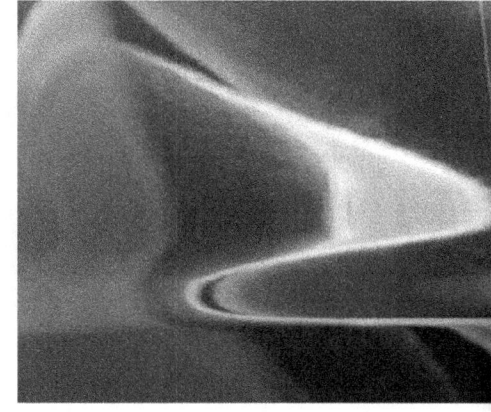

## claire's flash fiction

claire chose crazy

it was a lid she could sit on

after seven years, she got away with murder

claire flew to paris with dreams of    posing as a blue-eyed blonde
                                                    softly purring into gentlemen's ears
                                                    possessing the asylum of distance

but bitter, wild, and lonely have deep fangs

they     take hold
           gnaw incessantly
           refuse to let go

claire stripped to the bone    gray hair
                                  brown eyes
                                  murderer
                                hag

she marched    herself
                    *her true self*
                    to the top of the eiffel tower

finally

crazy

set free

## friday

addict
back at that sweet poison

bruised and abused
consenting
once again
to the abuser

love looks on
does not turn
away

fiercely guards
any tattered thread
of connection

in the distance
i hear a siren

closer to home
a hornet is
buzzing

building
its own
nest

## my idol

when i finally found her
she whispered—

think of your heart as the door
to an ornate birdcage

heavily draped
with Tibetan prayer flags

intentional flutters of
bright sky
and spacey blue

the windy white brush of
dragonfly wing

garnet
like the torch of
incense glow

the everything green
of soaking waters

and finally
mustard yellow
cupping a seed

these delicate
squares of cloth
guard and hold
the sacred portal

close your eyes
*cross your threshold*

what do you see
and smell

where do your
footsteps fall

is there sound
or taste

is your voice
your friend

allow your soul
the longest
linger—

this is home

now lift your eyelids
enter this room
with me

look closely
the latch is
tightly secured

those scraps of color
are discarded
twist ties

they rust and wear
melding doorjamb to
doorway in a
tireless fashion

it's like that
she said

## about this
## the thanks

to
Warren Publishing: Mindy Kuhn and Amy Ashby. thank you for the acknowledgement and the invitation.

The Writing Groups (especially the IWG, version.2014): your willingness to listen and critique (even when poetry wasn't your thing), speaks volumes regarding the kindness of your souls. i hope all of you keep writing.

Harley Gamble: special thanks for the great memory and muse of "claire's flash fiction."

Randy Siegel: i admire your confidence in dreams morphing into reality. thank you for your contagious inspiration and honest feedback. a necessary balance.

Mandy Thompson: my artist! you have shared your gift of the deep dive into thoughts, heart stories, and writing. thank you for helping me wrangle my words into clarity and tone.

Luciana Duce-Dugan: you are a fantastic teacher and mentor. your lessons on craft and intention still speak to me of confirmation and innovation. they have made the page stronger beneath my pen.

The Wee Poets Group: David Millman and Nancy Hatch Woodward. a seven-year (and counting) journey, together, down the rabbit hole of words, emotions, and imaginings—all while supporting each other through the doings of life.

David: you are generous and gentle with the words. your way with rhyme cannot be explained, only happily experienced.

Nancy: you are stalwart, supportive, and oh so forgiving of the weak moments. your voice often visits my page; a loving nudge of aspiration.

Barb: i don't know life without you. for this i am forever blessed and lucky.

Ron: i can't image life without you. for this i am forever blessed and loved.

www.ingramcontent.com/pod-product-compliance
Lightning Source LLC
Chambersburg PA
CBHW022109040426
42451CB00007B/195